Fact Finders®

Explore the Biomes

EXPLORE THE

Tropical Rain Forest

by Linda Tagliaferro

Consultant:
Dr. Sandra Mather
Professor Emerita of Geology and Astronomy
West Chester University
West Chester, Pennsylvania

Capstone press®

Mankato, Minnesota

Fact Finders is published by Capstone Press,
151 Good Counsel Drive, P.O. Box 669, Mankato, Minnesota 56002.
www.capstonepress.com

Library of Congress Cataloging-in-Publication Data
Tagliaferro, Linda.
   Explore the tropical rain forest / by Linda Tagliaferro.
   p. cm.—(Fact finders. Explore the biomes)
   Includes bibliographical references and index.
   ISBN-13: 978-0-7368-6407-7 (hardcover)
   ISBN-10: 0-7368-6407-5 (hardcover)
   ISBN-13: 978-0-7368-7510-3 (softcover pbk.)
   ISBN-10: 0-7368-7510-7 (softcover pbk.)
   1. Rain forest ecology—Juvenile literature. I. Title. II. Series.
QH541.5.R27T34 2007
577.34—dc22   2006004107

Summary: Discusses the plants, animals, and characteristics of the tropical rain forest biome.

Editorial Credits
Erika L. Shores, editor; Juliette Peters, designer; Tami Collins, map illustrator;
   Wanda Winch, photo researcher

Photo Credits
Corbis/Michael & Patricia Fogden, 14; zefa/PNC, cover (background)
Courtesy of Lawrence M. Kelly, 29
Courtesy of Linda Tagliaferro, 32
Creatas, 14 (scarab beetle)
Digital Vision/Gerry Ellis and Michael Durham, 3
Getty Images Inc./Stone/Art Wolfe, 26
James P. Rowan, 12
Minden Pictures/Frans Lanting, 13; Gerry Ellis, 6; Mark Moffett, 10–11; Michael & Patricia Fogden, 24
Peter Arnold/Friedrich Stark, 19; Heinz Plenge, 15; Kevin Schafer, 21; Luiz C. Marigo, 5, 25;
   Michael J. Balick, 20; Mike Kolloffell, 17; Ron Giling, 18, 22–23
Photodisc/Siede Preis, 1, 8 (palm frond); 6–7, 31 (bird of paradise); 25 (fern fronds)
Shutterstock, 9, 20 (pill bottle); Andreea Manciu, 18 (bananas); Foong Kok Leong, cover (foreground);
   Holger Wulschlaeger, 1, 4, 30 (butterfly); Jaana Piira, 27; Jostein Hauge, 19 (chocolate bar); Lisa F.
   Young, 11 (macaw); Rodney Lamirand, 23 (Brahma bull)

The author thanks Fabian Michelangeli, PhD, and George Shakespear of the New York Botanical
Garden; her husband, Fred Thorner, and son, Eric Thorner, for listening to all her stories about
rain forests.

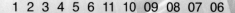

Table of Contents

CHAPTER 1

A Hot and Rainy Forest

The air is hot and muggy in this lush, green world. Heavy rain begins to fall. High above you, leafy branches of tall trees grow together to form a huge, green umbrella. Wide, waxy leaves and thick, tangled vines keep light from reaching the forest floor.

Bright blue butterflies and shiny hummingbirds flit through the trees. Parrots squawk, frogs croak, and furry monkeys howl. In this tropical rain forest millions of kinds of plants and animals, live together in a hot, wet **climate**.

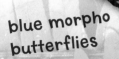

blue morpho
butterflies

Gigantic ferns are just a few of the lush, green plants that fill a rain forest with life.

The Tropical Rain Forest Biome

The world's tropical rain forests grow near the **equator**. Weather near the equator is usually warm and wet. Heat, daily rainfall, and lots of sunshine cause rain forests to burst with colorful flowers, tasty fruits, and tall trees.

Field Note

Where are tropical rain forests?

- Central America
- South America
- Africa
- southern Asia
- Australia

□ tropical rain forest

N
W—E
S

bird of paradise

A rain forest is a kind of **biome**. A biome is a community of certain types of plants and animals. All living things in a biome depend on each other and the climate to survive. Deserts, tundras, grasslands, and deciduous forests also are biomes. Each biome has a different climate and unique plants and animals.

CHAPTER 2

Layers of Life: Plants and Animals in the Tropical Rain Forest

Four layers of life are found in a tropical rain forest. In the **emergent layer**, giant treetops push their way toward the sun. These towering trees stick out far above the rest of the forest trees. Eagles and bats soar high above the treetops.

Below the emergent layer, trees grow in the rain forest **canopy**. In the canopy layer, millions of trees and other plants get plenty of sunshine and rain.

In the emergent layer, the very tallest trees tower above the rest of the forest.

9

Canopy plants and animals work together to survive. Air plants grow on tree branches to get sunlight and water. Rainwater forms little ponds inside these plants. The ponds make good homes for tadpoles.

Tiny ants live inside empty round spaces in ant plants. The ants lay eggs there and raise their young. If other insects or even large animals try to eat the plant, the ants sting them.

Unique rain forest ant plants are home to hundreds of the crawling insects.

Other animals live in the canopy, feasting on fruit, insects, and leaves. Monkeys swing from branches. Flying squirrels glide from tree to tree. Colorful macaws flock high in leafy branches.

macaw

Field Note

Macaws:

- **Size:** up to 39 inches (99 centimeters) long

- **Colors:** red, blue, yellow, green

- **Food:** use their beaks to crack open nuts and seeds

Field Note

Emerald tree boas live in the trees of the Amazon rain forest in South America.

- **Color:** green with white bands
- **Length:** 7 feet (2 meters) long
- **Food:** hunt at night for birds, rodents, and monkeys

Some dangerous animals travel between tall canopy trees and the **understory layer** of the tropical rain forest. Vine snakes look just like vines growing on trees. Their sharp fangs grab young birds and lizards. Emerald tree boas wrap themselves around branches and wait to attack birds, bats, and even monkeys.

Life on the Forest Floor

Where sunlight can't reach the forest floor, few plants can live. But mosses and **fungi** thrive on tree trunks and dead branches.

Other plants on the forest floor depend on animals to survive. The Rafflesia plant needs flies to spread its pollen. Rafflesia have the world's biggest flowers. The flowers stink like rotten meat. The smell attracts flies. Pollen sticks to the flies' bodies. When flies land on other Rafflesia flowers, they spread the pollen.

People might not want to get too close to the stinky Rafflesia flower, but flies can't stay away.

Animals on the forest floor are good at hunting in the dark. Ants and beetles tunnel through the soil to find food. Coral snakes, with bands of bright red, yellow and black, slither over the ground. They use their sense of smell to find **prey**. A bite from a coral snake is deadly to other animals.

scarab beetle

Bands of red, yellow, and black warn animals to stay away from the deadly coral snake.

The largest cat in South America's rain forests, the jaguar is a patient predator.

Large paw prints mark the damp soil. The prints belong to a large rain forest cat. A jaguar hides nearby. This spotted **predator** hunts for birds or monkeys that live higher in canopy trees. The jaguar leaps from its hiding place to catch its prey.

CHAPTER 3

People and the Tropical Rain Forest

Deep in the thick, green forest, noisy birds and howling monkeys fill the air with sounds. But animals aren't the only creatures living in the rain forest. Some native people live in tropical rain forests.

In South America's rain forests, the Huaorani people hunt and fish in traditional ways. They use blowguns with poison darts to hunt monkeys and other animals. Huaorani fishermen crush juice out of rain forest plants. When they pour the juice into a stream, fish die and float to the top. The fishermen collect the fish and eat them.

Some native people in the rain forest use blowguns to shoot poison darts at animals.

17

A woman uses a machete to cut away a pineapple growing on the ground.

Food from the Forest

Fish aren't the only food people find in the rain forest. Colorful fruits like yellow-orange papayas blossom here. The bright yellow bananas in the grocery store came from rain forest trees. Pineapples with their green, spiky tops sprout from rain forest soil. Jackfruits taste like bananas, but can weigh 80 pounds (36 kilograms) each.

bananas

Many people's favorite food and flavorings first came from the rain forest. Vanilla flavoring comes from the vanilla orchid's pods. Chocolate starts with beans from cacao trees. Spices like cinnamon, nutmeg, and allspice also are from rain forest plants.

chocolate bar

Medicine from the Forest

People in the rain forest are also looking for cures to diseases. The tropical rain forest is sometimes called the world's pharmacy. Many of the medicines people use today first came from leaves, bark, or other parts of rain forest plants. The cinchona tree's bark is made into quinine. Doctors use this drug to treat malaria, a sometimes deadly disease.

medicine

Grown in South America, the cinchona tree has bark that is made into the drug quinine.

Chemicals in the rosy periwinkle plant treat leukemia and other types of cancer.

Some scientists think certain rain forest plants, such as the rosy periwinkle, can help treat cancer. Ginger leaf juice helps sore throats to heal, and sticky gum from dragon's blood plants helps heal wounds.

FACT!

Curare is a large vine found in the rain forest canopy. In South America, curare is put on bruises and used to treat fevers and kidney stones.

People Change the Forest

People take other treasures besides food and medicine from the rain forests. After an ear-splitting boom, the ground shakes. Loggers chop down mahogany trees in the rain forest. Logging companies sell wood to make furniture.

Other companies cut down forests for use by people. Each year, millions of acres of rain forest land are cleared to make room for farms and ranches.

People clear huge areas of the rain forest to make room for ranches to raise livestock.

What will happen to the rain forest trees, plants, and animals? Rain forest animals lose their homes and food without the plants and trees. If the destruction of the rain forests continues, more than half of earth's plants and animals could disappear forever.

Brahma bull

23

Protecting the Rain Forest

Rain forests have more unique plants and animals than any other biome. What looks like a moving orchid is really an insect. Creeping nearby is a spider the size of a dinner plate. It can catch small birds. Tiny, brilliant orange toads swim in pools of water. Many people work to keep these rare animals from becoming **extinct**.

FACT!

Golden toads are just one of many rain forest animals being pushed toward extinction. Golden toads live in Costa Rica's rain forests. Due to logging and pollution, golden toads haven't been seen since the late 1980s.

People help preserve the rain forest by replanting trees.

People try to save rain forests by passing laws to protect them. In some rain forests, it is illegal to log or clear the land for farms. In other rain forests, the logging is controlled and trees are replanted.

Some plants can be harvested without harming the forest. People can help save rain forests by buying products made from these plants. In this way, people ensure that the rain forest will always be a lush home for millions of plants and animals.

CHAPTER 4

Tropical Rain Forest Field Guide

Where to find tropical rain forests:

Central America, South America, Africa, southern Asia, Australia

CLIMATE:

- warm and rainy
- average temperature: 68 to 93 degrees Fahrenheit (20 to 34 degrees Celsius)
- average rainfall: between 60 and 400 inches (152 and 1,016 centimeters) each year

INSECTS:

millions of species including ants, mosquitoes, termites, wasps, butterflies, cicadas

Question:

What are some ways people might study the insects and animals that live inside rain forest plants?

ANIMALS:

- **Common amphibians:** toads, poison arrow frogs, tree frogs
- **Common birds:** toucans, macaws, parrots, owls, eagles
- **Common mammals:** spider monkeys, sloths, ocelots, jaguars, howler monkeys
- **Common reptiles:** iguanas, chameleons, vine snakes, boa constrictors, coral snakes, crocodiles

PLANTS:

- **Common trees:** cacao trees, mahogany trees, rubber trees, kapok trees
- **Common plants:** orchids, philodendrons, rattans, lichens, mosses, ferns, strangler figs, lianas, bromeliads

Rain forest products: lumber, furniture, nuts, fruits, oils, rubber, medicine, cocoa beans

CHAPTER 5

A Scientist at Work

Fabian Michelangeli grew up in Venezuela in South America. Today, he works as a biologist for the New York Botanical Garden. He travels to rain forests to study ant plants. He photographs and collects the plants. In his laboratory, he dries the plants and puts them in sturdy folders. Michelangeli writes information about where and when he collected them.

Michelangeli files them in the botanical garden's herbarium, a library of 6 million plant samples. Other scientists use the herbarium to learn about rare or extinct plants. They'll find out which plants grow with other plants. They'll know which animals eat these plants. Michelangeli and other scientists will help make sure millions of kinds of plants can continue to thrive in the tropical rain forest biome.

FACT!

There are more than 3,000 plant "libraries" in the world. In the United States, there are more than 60 million samples of plants in 628 herbariums.

GLOSSARY

biome (BUY-ome)—an area with a particular type of climate, and certain plants and animals that live there

canopy (KAN-uh-pee)—the layer of leaves and branches formed by the tops of tall trees in a forest

climate (KLYE-mit)—the usual weather in a place

emergent layer (i-MUR-juhnt LAY-ur)—the top layer of a rain forest made up of the tallest trees

equator (i-KWAY-tur)—an imaginary line halfway between the North and South Poles; areas near the equator usually have a warm and wet climate.

extinct (ek-STINGKT)—no longer living anywhere in the world

fungus (FUHN-guhss)—a type of organism that has no leaves, flowers, or roots; mushrooms and molds are fungi.

predator (PRED-uh-tur)—an animal that hunts and eats other animals

prey (PRAY)—an animal hunted by another animal

understory layer (uhn-dur-STOR-ee LAY-ur)— the rain forest layer below the canopy; small trees, shrubs, and plants in the understory have large leaves to capture sunlight.

INTERNET SITES

FactHound offers a safe, fun way to find Internet sites related to this book. All of the sites on FactHound have been researched by our staff.

Here's how:

1. Visit *www.facthound.com*

2. Choose your grade level.

3. Type in this book ID **0736864075** for age-appropriate sites. You may also browse subjects by clicking on letters, or by clicking on pictures and words.

4. Click on the **Fetch It** button.

FactHound will fetch the best sites for you!

READ MORE

Castner, James L. *Surviving in the Rain Forest*. Deep in the Amazon. New York: Benchmark Books, 2002.

Hamilton, Jean. *The Secrets of Tropical Rainforests: Hot and Humid and Teeming with Life*. London Town Wildlife Series. Montrose, Calif.: London Town Press, 2005.

Hammerslough, Jane. *Into the Rain Forest*. New York: Scholastic, 2003.

INDEX

ABOUT THE AUTHOR

Linda Tagliaferro

Linda Tagliaferro is an award-winning author who lives in Little Neck, New York. She has written 28 books for children, young adults, and adults.

Linda has explored many tropical rain forests around the world. She speaks about her work at schools, libraries, and museums, such as The New York Hall of Science and New Jersey's Liberty Science Center. Her web site is www.lindatagliaferro.com.